# When God Equips a Writer

Moving Past Doubt

to

Embrace Your Writing Destiny

by Deanne Welsh

For every writer
who desires
to paint pictures with their pen.

For every reader
changed by the courage of a writer.

A single sentence or idea
can set people free.

# Acknowledgments

It takes a village to write a book and I am eternally
grateful for my village.

Thank you to Missie Richardson,
a wonderful counselor
who knows how to *Simplify Wisdom.*

Thank you to Nancy Booth,
a spiritual director, who expertly cultivated a sacred
space for me to connect with God.

Thank you to Pastor Jeff McAffee, whose messages
remind me to embrace God's destiny for my life.

The Unstoppable Writers community inspired me to
pen this message. We are a movement of writers
committed to God and one another's success.

A special thanks to my team of readers who gave me
invaluable feedback: Monica Vico, Sharon Martinez,
Ruth Deaton, Shelley Shaw, Lana Barnes, and Jenny
Wheeler. I could not have hit publish without you.

# Table of Contents

# INTRODUCTION

When God started nudging me to write this book, my heart paused. Was He sure? I thought I said all there was to say in *When God Calls a Writer*.

Writing books is more than simply typing words out on a page. The themes and lessons are slowly internalized if we let them sink below the surface of our lives. I've heard it said, the one spoken to is the one spoken through.

Our books transform us before they are released into the world to transform others.

If you have thought of giving up, this book is for you. It is for every writer living and writing in the gap between their dreams and current reality.

My prayer is that this book will equip you to persist on your writing journey and encourage you to continue believing in the possibility of the dreams God has given you.

Deanne Welsh

P.S. This book is about the winding path of growing into the writer you were created to be.

P.P.S. If you have only recently realized the call on your life to write, you may want to begin by reading book one in this series: *When God Calls a Writer.*

# Reading Tip

**Grab a pen and journal before you begin reading.**

I've set this book up to spark a conversation between you and God about your writing journey.

The paragraphs are short, so you have plenty of space to engage the ideas. Each section has a reflection and writing activity for you.

Some readers prefer buying a paperback or hardback to write in the book itself (because I've left space to do that), while others prefer the spaciousness of a personal notebook or journal.

Reflecting, having conversations, and implementing what we learn transforms us.

My hope is that you give yourself the gift of powerful pauses and intimate prayers.

God loves you.

He cares about your writing.

I am cheering you on,

Deanne

# Destiny

## Begin at the End

Chills swept over him. *It couldn't be. I dreamed of this moment twenty-two years ago.*

His hair stood on end. Their dialect and voices, familiar from years ago, haunted his dreams for years. Now they stood before him.

Breathless. Papa's eyes stared back at him from the face of a man he slowly recognized. *Reuben? Could it be?*

Emotion flooded his chest. He swallowed hard. *Don't let them see.* Memories flooded his mind: familiar streets, the scent of his mother's cooking, and the colorful cloak his father laid over his shoulders. *It's been so long. Do they know who I am?*

Fists clenched by his side, he gazed into the distance. *Hold it in. Don't let them see.* They knelt silently before him, as thousands of others had.

*God. Show me what to do. What does this mean? How can it be?*

This was the moment God promised and foretold in Joseph's childhood dreams. It was ordained and determined before he was born. The childhood dream was more than a dream. It was a promise and a prophecy calling forth and highlighting what God had already ordained for him.

God's whispers to him in the dark of the night and the prison cell were true. All the years of wondering if his vision meant anything and if events could have turned out differently suddenly melted away.

The cords of his life came together, and even that which was meant to harm him, the gut-wrenching betrayal of his brothers and the spiteful deceit of a woman, faded away in the light of God's glory and goodness.

Gratitude filled his heart. Those dark moments still stung and could have easily brought death, but instead, God took the enemy's attempt to bring death and used it for good.

To outsiders, the moment was meaningless, but to the man—who endured a pit, slavery, prison, and more—this moment was a holy confirmation of the destiny God had prophesied when he was a boy.

Joseph, a man at the height of success, leadership, and power, stood before his brothers deciding whether to spare the life of the sojourners who had come looking for relief and food.

For years, Joseph interpreted the dreams of others, and now his dream was being interpreted in the flesh, right before his eyes. Joseph's entire world shifted, seeing his brothers kneeling before him. *Could this be a divine homecoming and the fulfillment of my destiny?*

The fame and wealth were nice, but he was haunted by a longing for his father and mother, wondering if his brothers regretted their actions.

Just like when God planned salvation before Adam and Eve sinned, He prepared a way forward for Joseph before his brothers betrayed him.

Every moment of Joseph's long and winding journey was held in the loving hands of the Father.

If God gave me the initial dream and I got to plot Joseph's twenty-two-year plan, it would include training, mentorship by his father, and growing responsibilities at home. I would not have chosen the path or epic story God chose for Joseph.

I wish there was a blueprint for writers. If only God gave us a dream, and then boom, fulfillment happened in one smooth, seamless process. But this is not a true story.

God is a masterful storyteller; He wove all the pieces of Joseph's life and disparate seasons together: seamlessly and perfectly. He wants to do the same with the story of your life and the poems, stories, songs, or curriculum that you are writing.

Will you journey with me through these pages? Will you trust God with the pieces of your own life and writing journey?

It's okay to bring your doubt and discouragement along for the ride. God welcomes each of our emotions and the totality of who we are, right here, right now.

Joseph did not foresee this tangible moment of being reunited with his brothers at the beginning of his life. All he had was a temporal dream that God etched into his memory and heart.

A dream is where our own story often begins.

Are you ready?

Your "yes" changes everything.

# Begin with a Dream

He woke up with a start and stared into the darkness of the night. *Was that real or just a dream?* Silence, save the quiet breathing of his brothers, greeted his thoughts. Taking a deep breath, the image of his brother bowing before him was seared into his mind, beckoning him into a mysterious future.

It captivated his imagination and he struggled to fall back asleep. Staring at the ceiling of the tent, he tried to quiet his breathing. *What does it mean? Was it from God?*

*I've never had a dream like that.* He felt known, called, trusted, and anointed. It was different from how he typically felt: beloved by his father but despised by his brothers. Every effort he made to win them over was met with disdain. They would never treat him as an equal, as they were too steeped in their mother Leah's hurt and resentment of their father's favoritism of Joseph and his mother, Rachel.

He felt lonely even though he often took advantage of his father's doting affection.

Dreams change everything and God's dreams for us open us to new possibilities and an identity that is often different from how we see ourselves.

Do you have dreams like this? Thoughts of the future that light you up and fill you with excitement and hope?

Did you know that most inventions and significant breakthroughs start with a vision that shifts and shakes things up?

We feel the truth of these moments in our bones and the deep inner places of our hearts.

Dreams can awaken us as they shift our perspective to something new or previously hidden. The first step for us is to pause and ask God about the dreams He has for us, and to be honest in the dreams we hold protectively to our chests. If we never articulate or take the time to receive the vision and dream, we wander aimlessly without a clear picture to guide us forward.

My process for unearthing the dreams God has given me includes the practice of Listening Prayer (see *When God Calls a Writer*), morning pages, counseling, spiritual direction sessions, walking in nature, learning to be honest with myself, and more.

Now it's your turn.

What dreams God has placed in your heart? Take a moment to ask Him to reveal them and then *write them down*.

If we write ourselves task lists or grocery lists to remember important things, how much more vital is it to write down the pictures, impressions, and words we hear from God?

This, right now, is your moment to pause and listen.

# Disaster

## Critics

When we first receive a dream, we are often as excited and invigorated as Joseph was. As we begin to move forward, this is important to remember:

When God gives you a vision or dream for your future, it is yours. There may be friends or family who catch a glimpse of the vision, too, but sadly, there are people who will not.

God-given dreams don't always make sense to others because of the gap between the dream and our day-to-day reality. Sadly, there are people who will mock and criticize our dreams because they do not understand. Unfortunately, there are those who may   try to discourage or dissuade you from pursuing your dream by saying things like, "You are not good enough," and "That's not realistic."

Dreams rarely fit our current situation. When we share them, others may perceive the dream as crazy or full of pride without realizing that each of us was created by God to grow and develop. Who we are today is not who we will be tomorrow, or for the rest of eternity.

Perhaps the loudest critics are not people, but the sound of our own thoughts and fears.
Who am I to write this book? Why did God *call* me? Did He make a mistake?

Our dreams have the potential to threaten others because they have suppressed their own God-given dreams or because the vision disrupts their view of who we are and how our relationship with them currently works.

At other times, our dreams scare us because we attach expectations and tasks to them, feeling the weight of trying to bring them to fulfillment in our own strength and time.

The gap is what makes it a dream and not a current reality.

If you are feeling the tension of living in the gap, know that you are not alone. Countless others have stood in this luminal space, the time between today and the not yet here.

God meets us in the gap.

The choice is up to us. Will we trust God with the dreams and the gap, or will we try to bridge it on our own through striving, perfectionism, and stress?

I've tried both ways and there is only one that brings the wonder, freedom, and strength I desperately long for in my creativity and writing.

Your turn.

Take a moment to list out the outer and inner critics and lies you are facing in your creative and writing journey. What's holding you back from trusting God with the gap between your dreams and your day-to-day reality?

# Betrayed

Joseph stared up at the empty sky as the voices of his brothers receded and their laughter drifted down to him.  Struggling to breathe, the sting of betrayal wrapped itself around his chest, crushing him. *How did this happen? Why?*

While I have never sat at the bottom of a physical pit, I have found myself crushed and brought exceedingly low by circumstances and people. Sometimes the pit has nothing to do with people or circumstances, but rather with the lies and stories I tell myself about them, such as no one will ever love me, I don't deserve good things, I'm not good enough, etc.

The pit feels like the antithesis of our dreams. Instead of the honor and respect that were so palpable in his dream, Joseph sat surrounded by dirt and the growing dark and cold as night fell.

The dream was not given to his brothers. They did not see the destiny God had for Joseph. Others will not always see the dreams burning inside your chest, or the gifts slowly sprouting inside longing to be noticed and nurtured.

Others may even betray or disbelieve your God-given dreams. This often happens as they are just beginning to emerge because we long for confirmation and affirmation from those around us.

Sometimes we look to the right people who have the vision to see the possibility of our dreams too. Other times, we put our trust in teachers or parents who are blind to the dream and all the yet-to-be-revealed strengths glimmering beneath the surface of who we are today.

Try as they might (and sadly, some do not try), they do not see the reality. Worse yet, they may project their hurt, fear, and distorted thinking onto you. Your dream is not possible, or perhaps, you don't have what it takes.…

These voices and wounds cut deep. Countless writers are chained by these inaccuracies about their identity and potential.

Who will we trust: the gut instinct God has placed within us and the dreams burning in our hearts, or the narrow vision of a critic?

No one is born a great writer. Writing is a muscle that each and every one of us can strengthen.

Let's make room for the voices of truth: God's voice about who we are and the inner knowing He has placed within us. That voice within, deep in our bones, that knows we were made to string words together.

It takes tremendous courage and tenacity to begin walking and working in the direction of our dreams. They often stretch us beyond our current capability and invite us to deeper places of trust and commitment.

Are there lies or wounds from past critics that have crippled you? What can you do to combat them with God's truth about your identity and His love for you?

Brainstorm a list. A few of my favorite ways are writing verses on notecards that I put in my car, bathroom, and office so that I am reminded of the truth.

# Disruption

## Disintegration

It's one thing to sit in a pit close to home where everything is familiar and safe (even if the pit is not). The coins jingled as they passed from the slaveholder's hands to those of his brothers. *My brother just enslaved me and gave my life away. What now?*

The path of his life seemed to disintegrate in a single moment of gut-wrenching betrayal. Pulled up from the pit, he trudged behind swaying camels. Dust coated his face and throat as the rhythms, land, and people of his life faded into the distance.

*Where are we going? What is to become of me? God! God! Please let my father figure out what happened and come to save me. Help me!*

Did he remember the dream and cling to hope despite racing thoughts?

Often, it's easier to see the goodness and guidance of God in hindsight. Looking back, we notice the helping hand, the cup of water in the desert.

Joseph's story invites us to be honest with God, like the Psalmists. God is big enough to hear and handle our anger, grief, joy, and more!

So often we are like a caterpillar hanging from a leaf painstakingly shedding its skin to reveal a chrysalis. The story of this creature is not over yet. The season for emerging as a new creation and spreading your wings is coming.

Are you in an uncomfortable season, staring at the sky from the bottom of a pit...?

You are not alone!

In our pit experiences, we feel shaken and smashed. It may feel as though our very identity is being torn to shreds.

It's hard to type this. I have not been enslaved or stuck at the bottom of a pit. But looking back, I see tortuous moments in my own life. There have been long seasons and weeks where I have felt destitute and deeply discouraged.

I've sat alone, sobbing into my pillow, because I felt unseen, invisible, and unimportant. The circumstances matter less than the impact of those devastating moments. The pain of letting go and wondering who I am.

I've sat in the passenger seat of a car in my twenties, staring out the window, wondering why I burned out in teaching and if there was a career or future for me. Even the thought of flipping hamburgers at a fast-food restaurant felt like too much to handle.

I have been mushed up and pummeled, felt forgotten by those I left behind as they moved on in their lives, and I continue to wrestle with lingering loneliness and feeling like an outsider.

The story of Joseph comforts me because I know I am not alone. In those moments of being betrayed, sold, and forgotten…God was with Joseph. Even when everything familiar was crushed and the dream became an impossibility by the world's standards

The story was not over.

Where are you today? Perhaps you felt the call and nudge of God to write and so you began, filled with passion and purpose.

But now…perhaps it hasn't been going as you expected. Perhaps the marketing is draining your energy and you feel like the dream would require someone different from who you are….

Perhaps you are busy mothering, working, or simply surviving.

You need to know this:

Your story is not over. This is a single chapter and not a decree on how your life will be for the next fifty or even five years.

Just as the legacy of Joseph was not his time in the pit, this season does not define you or determine your creative destiny.

Take a breath.

Allow the sorrow to pour from your eyes, heart, and pen. Do not mourn alone. Find safe people who understand. Give yourself space to grieve and pour out your heart to God.

Your story is only beginning and beginnings are hard.

Do not give up.

Some of my most powerful moments with God have been when I allowed my unbridled grief to flow, sobbing in His presence.

Those moments of naked vulnerability sometimes ushered me into the powerful and kind presence of God. While an answer or immediate solution did not emerge, I felt God whispering, "I see you. You are not alone. I am with you in this."

The tears flowed all the harder because I suddenly knew that God can handle all my anger, hate, fear, anxiety, and depression.

We don't have to protect Him by pretending we are fine or minimizing the pain we feel. It doesn't matter if the cause of the grief is a small or significant issue in the eyes of the world.

God made your heart and the breadth of your emotional landscape.

What season are you in today? Is there anything you need to grieve and pour out to God?

## In Between

As we read about Joseph's life, there is so much left to the imagination. What happened between his desolation in the pit and becoming Potiphar's right-hand man?

Similarly, you may feel overlooked and hidden in certain seasons of your life. Perhaps your writing does not have the space you crave as you juggle a new baby or the responsibility of caretaking for a loved one.

The gap in Joseph's story in Scripture can remind us that even in the seeming distances from our dreams, even in the midst of the routine and mundane, God is with us.

Perhaps you've wondered as I have: Are our dreams just pipe dreams? Are the visions etched on our hearts really from Him?

The freedom truth is this:

The childhood dreams that feel as though they have drifted off like clouds, God holds us and the desires of our hearts close. If something is precious to us, we can trust God with it.

We can trust Him with every dream and desire.

Joseph's journey reminds us that God knows our dreams and visions. He crafted our hearts and wrote our stories long before we took our first breath.

During in-between seasons, the words God continues to give me are

Rest

Wait

Trust.

I don't love these words.

Instead, I long for God to tell me to move and make something happen. These words feel passive, and yet, over the years and countless luminal spaces, I have found that they are the opposite.

Rest is active. It opens room for me to heal, grow, and connect with God in deeper ways.

Waiting is expectant; I watch for what God is doing.

Trust wraps me in quiet confidence. I know my story is not over.

Trust is not static. It can wax and wane, and I've often found comfort in the prayer: Help my unbelief!

As a writer in a season of waiting, these are the times
when I struggle:

- Where will I focus?
- What will I write?
- What's the point?
- Why me?

My best advice to myself and to others is to write
gently and to keep goals small and simple.

The practice of morning pages (page 72) is one of my
favorite ways to keep writing consistent and feeling
light. First introduced to me by Julia Cameron's books,
this daily writing rhythm keeps me anchored and
provides a safe space to process, reflect, and grow.

A few other examples of small and simple goals that
keep me connected to my pen are

- having a goal of writing five minutes a day,

- keeping a small notebook in my purse to jot
  down ideas as they come, and counting it as my
  writing for the day, and

- having a goal of writing a single line or sentence
  a day.

If words are not flowing freely because of a difficult season, you could even borrow the words of others for your writing. Jot down a favorite quote or create a vision board of inspiring pictures and words from a magazine.

Our view of writing is often narrow and all it takes is a moment to switch our perspective and embrace all the words always dancing within and around us.

As writers, we live in the space in between our ethereal ideas and bringing them to life on paper.

My best advice is to start where you are, with what you have, because it is enough for your next step forward.

Aim for consistent forward motion but know that so much of our writing is done before our pens hit the paper. As you go about your life, stories and insights are being written on your heart and in your life.

Don't discount small beginnings (Zech. 4:10).

The story of the widow providing food for Elijah in 1 Kings 17 has encouraged me during hard seasons when my writing was relegated to the cracks and crevices of my life.

As Elijah approaches the widow for food, she shakes her head in disbelief: "I barely have enough to eat one last meal with my son before we die."

And yet…God!

As creatives, we can feel burned out and barren.

In these seasons we have a choice: Will we bring our meager supplies to God? Will we trust Him in the midst of our daily responsibilities to carry and birth the creative ideas He has woven into the very fabric of our beings?

When I was amid an in-between season and discouragement had settled into my bones, I was sitting in a worship service. My desires were clear but the path forward felt heavy, impossible, and slow.

God planted a picture in my mind: my dreams and visions were in a white-knuckle clutch to my chest. Fear pulsed through my body and I held others at a distance. Experiences from my childhood influenced my stance, those moments when I felt unsafe, overlooked, and ignored.

I built a self-protective wall around the things I cared most about. Were others trustworthy, let alone God? Would they care about and protect my writing dreams the way I did?

In that moment, God revealed my spiritual posture and the ways I was keeping everyone at bay, struggling under the weight of my creative destiny, all alone.

*It doesn't have to be this way,* He gently whispered.

*I give you visions and dreams.*

*Will you trust me to show you what I have for you, and to release back to me any that are not for you, or not for this season?*

*I created you with your unique and specific gifts, perspective, and personality.*

*Will you let me carry them?*

*Will you let me guide and direct your creative destiny?*

The soft questions blew over my soul and I wept.

Relief swept over me. I didn't have to carry, protect, and fulfill my destiny alone.

God wants to carry and protect you and the dreams you've squirreled away, stuffing them into the shadows, pretending they don't exist.

You can open your hands, look up, and let your dreams fly back into the capable hands of the One who placed them within your chest. Take a moment to do that now.

<hr>

A poem back to you, from God's heart:

Listen,

close your eyes,

and allow me to paint and speak vibrant alive words

in your heart and soul and

to whisper songs and poetry in your ears.


Then, take a moment to pause,

holding them close and dear.

Allow me to shape your life and the gifts I have given you,

and then open your hands and

allow them to fly, soar, and dance into the world.


This is our rhythm, connection, and dance.

You are the King's artist and scribe.

I am your patron, your guide, your mentor, and your muse.


Listen to me and I will guide you all the days of your life.

<hr>

# Destination?

## Stepping Stones

Again, while there is nothing written about the gap between Joseph being sold into slavery and then serving as the second-in-command in Potiphar's household, we can look back over his story and see how God was with Joseph every step of the way.

Somehow, Joseph made it from the pit to the position of trusted steward of all that Potiphar possessed. His character, strengths, and skills were noticed at the appointed time. Joseph stepped from the constraints of chains to being entrusted with more than he thought possible.

I wonder if Joseph thought Potiphar's house was the fulfillment of God's promise to him: leadership, prestige, and respect were his.

It's easy to mistake a stepping stone for a destination.

If you're like me, change is hard and I often want to build a permanent home on a stepping stone to stay comfortable.

It's painful to let a good thing go and trust God as I step into the unknown. Even worse is when I'm thrust into the unknown by a circumstance outside my control.

Life is constantly changing, and yet, God invites us to make HIM our permanent home.

Take a minute to reflect on where you are right now. Is this season or position a stepping stone?

How will you trust God with today and your future?

## Derailed

When Joseph was again confronted by Potiphar's wife, he stood strong. *No! I could never betray the trust of Potiphar.* Unfortunately, William Congreve had it correct: *Hell hath no fury as a woman scorned.*

Potiphar's wife took Joseph's rejection and created a lie to damage his destiny. Joseph is yanked from his prestigious position and thrown into prison.

Can you relate? Maybe not to prison, but to those moments that blindside us, sweeping us off our feet and landing us in the dust and discouragement of a dark night.

Satan wants nothing more than to distort and destroy who God made you and what God has prepared in advance for you to do. Satan may even try to stir up people and circumstances to derail us. Perhaps there are distorted thoughts and lies He suggested long ago that you believe even though they are chaining you to a false identity.

Don't worry, your story does not end with these moments. It's important not to skip them. Sometimes these dark moments can become the most transforming ones of our stories.

The Bible we hold in our hands is the work of writers and scribes who were faithful to write what the Holy Spirit placed on their hearts.

The stories we feel most connected to are those that include difficulty and trials.

When we share our moments of brokenness and how God brought us through, we encourage and equip others to keep moving forward. The ripple effect of our words is beyond what we can imagine.

Writing preserves our stories and gives us the ability to share them, for hundreds and even thousands of years. Stringing sentences together can be an act of faith, and our pens can offer hope and help to others.

This is why Satan will often try to discourage you as a writer. If he can get you to stop writing, to stop using the very tool that sets YOU and others free…then he not only wins at this moment, but he holds back the very words that could impact people for years to come.

Read that again.

Your writing is not just about today, or the book you hope to publish by the end of the year.

God can use your words to impact people for hundreds and even thousands of years to come. Just pick up your Bible and imagine if Satan had managed to derail all those writers. I'm sure he tried to.

Not only are we contending for our writing on a daily basis, but even wonderful opportunities can present new challenges and disappointments to overcome.

Joseph was not protected from the schemes of Potiphar's wife despite Potiphar's favor resting on his every decision.

When we encounter life-changing events, it is hard to trust anyone, especially God. Our health, home, and relationships may hang in the balance.

Sometimes there are often no words to assuage our fears or comfort our hearts in the midst of trauma and pain. And yet, Joseph's story reminds us that God is not done writing our story.

Some of us will receive the fulfillment, or partial fulfillment, of our dreams on earth, while others will only glimpse them in the distance as Moses did standing on the mountain overlooking the Promised Land.

Creating something out of nothing is not easy. Don't give up.

Don't let your discouragement determine your destiny.

Discouragement is something we all struggle with from time to time. Don't face it alone!
This is why having positive and encouraging friends is so important! Do you have a writing community or friends who support your writing journey?

Jot down a list of your community and friends who support your writing journey. Include ideas for other places you can continue building your support and connections.

Don't be discouraged if it takes you a while to find your flock. When I began my writing journey, I had to look online for writerly friendships and connections. It's why I created a free Facebook group for writers: **Unstoppable Writers**.

We are stronger together.

# Dark Night

## Abandoned

Joseph sighed and leaned against the wall of the prison cell. Night fell, and the small space felt familiar. The damp smell of dirt brought him back to all those years ago when he lay weeping at the bottom of the pit.

A sharp sting traveled from his chest and up his throat. It was hard to accept the change from trusted confidant to criminal. *Surely Potiphar knew the truth.* Pressing his eyes closed, he felt the truth. *I would be dead if Potiphar believed his wife's lies.*

*Innocent. Persecuted. Betrayed.* The refrain reverberated in his head. Opening worried eyes, he breathed the words that first left his lips in the pit all those years ago and had continued to serve as his refrain ever since:

*God, help me. Have mercy on me. My life is in your hands. There is nothing I can do to fix or change this situation. Thank you for being with me. Please grant me your peace and protection.*

Perhaps, as his prayers filled the prison cell, a new refrain emerged in his spirit:

*I have been here before. This place feels familiar. God, you raised me up. Help me trust you to do it again.*

Joseph fell into a light sleep. A few minutes later, the head of the guards made his rounds and paused in front of Joseph's cell.

Gazing at the newest prisoner, accused of trying to rape a woman, he felt something stir in his gut. *This man did not look like an assailant. Instead, he seemed wrapped in a soft peace.*

Curiosity took root in the head guard. *I must talk to him tomorrow.* It would not have been the first time that an innocent person was imprisoned at the whim of the wealthy.

On our darkest nights, we often don't see the hand of God moving on our behalf. Sometimes we experience His peace and comfort, and other times we may feel as though our prayers reverberate off the walls surrounding us.

Hindsight can offer us a new perspective if we allow it to. Zora Neale Hurston said it beautifully, "There are years that ask questions and years that answer."

Pause for a moment and imagine Joseph sitting in the prison cell, completely boxed in and helpless. Write down a word or phrase to capture the times you have felt similarly:

Sometimes, these desert seasons and moments are devastating and obvious, other times they are subtle, and we feel ourselves deflating like a balloon losing air. Perhaps we wake up one day realizing we are depressed and have lost our joy.

Every moment matters to God. Take a couple of minutes to notice any areas where you feel discouraged.

## Reality

I wonder if Joseph sensed his time in prison was a season. When we realize that a place or position is a stepping stone, it is easier to hold it lightly, no longer letting it define us or dictate our future.

Did Joseph count the passing months, wondering when the season would end?

I know I do.

While I typically stuff down my thoughts and feelings that God should hurry up, He sees my heart screaming, *Why is it taking so long? Please make it happen NOW!*

A wise counselor (thank you, Missie Richardson!) encouraged me to ask God,

> "What is the race you have for me to run today?
> The race for this season?"

These questions opened a door for me. I sat with the questions for days and months, allowing God to speak to my heart.

Realizing that my life is not just a single long race but a series of relays and parts allowed me to acknowledge the seasons of waiting, feeling imprisoned, and those of being elevated and fulfilled dreams.

The internal pressure I felt lifted.

I did not need to rush or push toward achieving the dreams God placed in my heart. I could rest in Him, wait on Him, and trust Him to make my steps clear: for today, this week, this month, this season, and beyond.

The beauty of these questions is their acknowledgment of the many roles and seasons contained in a single life.

What are some of the races or seasons you have experienced in the last ten years?

# Sinking

What if Joseph had wallowed in self-pity in prison? It's easy to look down and inward when something bad happens, especially if it is unfair and unjust. The circumstances may feel like an open invitation to sink into victimhood and wait for someone else to make it right.

While we don't know Joseph's exact course of action, we find him a few verses later, finding favor with the prison guard and serving his fellow inmates.

Do we have the courage to do the same?

Are we willing to surrender and fully experience the broken areas of desolation? God is big enough to handle our grief and we are in good company when we learn to lament: David, Job, Rachel…every person encounters loss and hardship.

What if we lifted our tear-stained faces to Jesus, poured out our hearts to Him, and then patiently waited for the path to be made clear?

Scripture doesn't include the details of Joseph's breakthrough moments: the first conversation between him and the warden, what serving was like, or how he stayed faithful in the midst of it all.

Instead, we have only a few verses and it gives us a glimpse into the spirit of Joseph and his willingness to serve.

God did the work within Joseph in the quiet of his cell and prepared him for the work within the entire prison.

Have you had prison-like seasons? Where you felt badgered, unjustly persecuted, or perhaps overlooked and invisible?

Jot down a few.

Your story is not over.

Give yourself time to peel back any new layers of grief about the moments you jotted down. Remember, healing is a journey and recursive.

Whenever you are ready (and you may return to this time and time again), pause in silence and gently look up at the face of Jesus, simply basking in His presence.

Allow Him to see you in the fullness of who you are and all you have experienced — no more hiding.

Read Matthew 11:28–29 and take some time to savor Jesus' invitation to us: *Come to me, all you who are weary and burdened, and I will give you rest.*

As you sit in God's loving presence, begin to look around and notice how He is already at work in your life and your writing journey.

Pause to remember all He has brought you through and the ways in which you have experienced Him along the way.

## Divine Delays

The very experience of being betrayed and cast down brought Joseph into the presence of the king's servants.

When two of the king's servants needed an interpreter for their dreams, God prepared Joseph and placed him in the right place to assist them.

I wonder if Joseph saw the cupbearer elevated and eagerly awaited word that he was being released. The cupbearer promised to remember and assist Joseph.

Hours ticked by, then days, weeks, and two long years.

Surely the promise made in the depths of the prison was forgotten. It seemed that the door of opportunity and freedom were nailed shut forever.

I don't know if Joseph felt this way, but I have.

When God's promise delays or the clear vision begins to feel distant and unattainable, I find myself sinking into doubt, questioning, and even despair.

Writing is a long game, my friends.
We want to finish one project or book and instantly be catapulted to fame. Perhaps those who ardently promised to support and promote your work have forgotten and found other pursuits or interests.

How will we respond?

We can whither and set aside our vision, hopes, and dreams. The only other option is to buckle down, not by striving, but with patience and persistence.

No one can tell you whether you are unstoppable. It is a choice.

Will you continue to create space to write and grow?

Will you water the seeds of creativity within your chest?

While we do not hear much about Joseph in the years of waiting, I like to imagine him serving faithfully while also pouring out his heartache and frustration to God.

"Let us not become weary in doing good, for at the proper time we will reap a harvest if we do not give up" (Gal. 6:9 NIV).

We all have hard and discouraging days. Times when we stop our labor and lie exhausted on the desert floor of our lives.

Will we look up and allow God to feed and sustain us, gently nursing us back to health, as He did for Elijah? Sometimes the best thing we can do for our writing and spiritual journey is to stop, eat, and take a nap.

It may include calling a friend to confess your discouragement and ask for prayer, or even going to the movies and giving yourself a break from the high expectations you have for yourself.

How will you allow God to replenish you this week?

Write it down and actively create space for it.

Living in the tension of unfulfilled desires and dreams
is not for the faint of heart. Rather, we go through a
continual process of releasing our grief and dreams to
God and receiving His comfort and strength.

One day at a time, Joseph lived through the years of
waiting.

If you are in a season of waiting, look to the One who
knew you before you were formed in your mother's
womb or took your first breath. He sees you and knows
you, including the desire to write and make a
difference.

Here's a poem from my good friend and author Lisa
Kurz Parrish that I've found helpful to pray:

You are calling, and I am listening.
Lead me deeper into You.
Remind me that I can do nothing without You.
Open my ears to hear the words You want me to write.

I invite you into my writing, my imagination, my
dreams, and my hopes.

Fuel my passion as only You can.
You are the creative spark within me.

Come. Teach me.
I am listening.

Joseph's story reminds us that God is on the move and never caught by surprise. As long as you are alive, your story is not done yet.

If you find yourself in the middle of a divine delay, look for small ways to start using your gifts and making pieces of your dream a reality, unless of course, God is nudging you to wait.

Our efforts may feel as small as a mustard seed and yet, God delights in shaping us and our gifts into so much more than we could have asked or imagined.

Below are a few of the gifts I have found during seasons of waiting and delay. These seasons

- create space to slow down,
- deepen my understanding of myself and my dreams,
- act as a time for pruning when I realize what needs to be let go and what is truly important,
- fuel my deepest longings,
- strengthen my commitment to do whatever it takes to fulfill the dream, and
- encourage me to connect with others because we were not meant to walk through desert seasons alone.

Even as we embrace these gifts, it's good to remember that these seasons are not our final destination.

Are you prepared to learn from the season you are in while remaining open to God's divine winds of change?

Your story is not over and God still holds the pen.

Proverbs 16:1–9 offers a powerful reminder and promise. We make plans and yet, it is God who chooses our steps.

Reflect on how God has orchestrated the path of your life up to this moment.

What are some of the dreams and plans you have for the future? Don't be afraid to dream with God!

Write them down and spend some time inviting God to continue guiding your steps.

# Dawn

## The Chosen

The despised youngest brother, mocked for being a dreamer, became a sought-after dream interpreter for the king.

Stepping into our divine destiny is not about changing who we are, although we can shift and mature over time. It is resting in our connection with God and allowing Him to reveal who He created us to be.

The very gift Joseph freely shared in the prison became the key to his freedom and entrance into the king's court.

When we hoard our gifts and hide them out of fear of failure or criticism, we may be delaying the destiny God has for us.

Share your gifts! Shine your light. As writers, God gives us ideas, stories, and words that impact us and that can impact others if we are willing to share them.

Stepping into our divine destiny is a journey of faithfulness and patience, staying close to the One who made us.

We don't need to fight for our dreams alone; God's got a better plan. Allow Him to guide your steps through every adversity and opportunity because He has promised to be there every step of the way.

We are often blind to our own gifts and talent. We struggle trying to figure out how our diverse desires and passions meld together into a cohesive whole.

God's got this!

He knows every chamber of your heart and chapter of your story. Will you let Him hold the pen and guide your steps?

What often begins in private, hearing and connecting with God, can encourage and equip us to take bold steps in public.

As Joseph stepped into the court of the king, the challenges were not over. Each part of our life on earth carries with it unique doubts and burdens.

I've learned that I cannot face my struggles alone and am incredibly thankful for praying friends, a safe counselor to process with, and my spiritual director, Nancy Booth, who creates a sacred space for me to be honest and still in God's presence.

My view of my dreams for years was that everything would become easier as they came to fruition. This has not been the case.

So many of my dreams have been fulfilled:

- I am typing this in the room dedicated to my writing and work, the one I wished for over a decade.
- I am thankful for four books published (this is my fifth) when years ago, I wondered how to even begin the process.
- Yes, I am excited to live in a world of words as I work on my projects and equip authors and nonprofits to market themselves effectively.

And yet, there are other dreams drumming in my chest that feel so far away, and I sometimes wonder if they will ever come true.

All the encouragement and reminders within the pages of this book are for me too. It is not easy to persist as a writer.

I was not expecting to write a follow-up book to *When God Calls a Writer*, and yet, it makes sense.

The call is the first step when we hear and respond to God's invitation to write.

Then begins the long and tedious journey of being faithful to continue saying YES to the invitation. We need God to equip us.

Each day brings unique challenges, and on my best days, I am honest enough to admit it and ask for God's help and the help of those around me.

Joseph could not meet the challenge of God's calling in his own strength. Only God could supply the relationships and interpretation of Pharaoh's dream that would bring about the fulfillment of Joseph's.

Did Joseph's skin shiver, knowing how much was on the line? Did he take a deep breath and pray feverishly, or simply let go and trust?

How are you feeling about your dreams and their fulfillment? God welcomes the range of your emotions and the fact that many of them are constantly shifting.

## The Choice

Your "yes" changes everything.

Joseph could have allowed the prison to become an integral part of his identity. Instead, he released it back to God along with his prison garments and put on fresh clothes before entering the king's presence.

How often do we cling to the rags of past writing seasons, or allow the doubts and lies to call the shots in our lives?

Saying "yes" is realizing that you and your circumstances cannot stay the same and accepting responsibility for your part in the transformation.

Caterpillars are my favorite illustration of this. The process of change to become a butterfly is gruesome and messy. Every time I see a butterfly on my morning walk, I am reminded that although change is painful, God can use it for good in my life and the lives of others.

Could Joseph have stayed in prison?

Probably not without dire consequences for disobeying the king. But how often do we delay, doubt, or distract ourselves from obeying the summons of our eternal King?

Is God calling you to step out in your writing?




Will you say yes?

## The Challenge

Joseph woke up, stretched, and prepared for his regular duties assisting the prison warden. Little did he know that everything would change in an instant.

How often have you found this to be true?

Sometimes change comes slowly and other times, it happens in the snap of a second. The king summoned Joseph to come and interpret his dream.

Imagine if Joseph had simply set up shop in the pit and ignored the invitation of the king because he thought he had "arrived" and was meant to stay in the prison forever.

We were not made for prison. God has so much more for us.

Before Joseph could step out of the prison, some things needed to change.

He was required to discard his prison clothes, wash, shave, and put on new clothes worthy of the king's palace and presence.

When the door of possibility beckons us, offering gentle or loud invitations to move forward, we too must pause to release what no longer fits and receive all that will prepare us to move forward.

We cannot walk through open doors carrying
everything from the last season in our arms. We will
not fit.

When God beckons us to grow and step into new
responsibilities or leadership, there are thoughts,
behaviors, and yes, even physical clothing and spaces
we must release.

The same is true when God asks us to step down, take
on a smaller role, or begin again when we have toiled
so hard to be where we are.

It can be hard to let go. Give yourself space to grieve
and process the losses even as you begin to step into
the new. Letting go precedes receiving.

Perhaps, in the midst of releasing, God is offering you
the new clothing of

forgiveness

humility

trust

grace

patience

…and more.

While we may like the idea of putting on expensive clothes, Jesus is different from earthly kings.

Sometimes God's "higher" is "lower" by the world's standards. He invites us to take a servant's robe and wash the feet of our brothers and sisters. Are we willing to serve with our words and writing, regardless of the impact and how many copies we sell?

It's not an easy question to answer. I return to it time and time again, as God gently invites me to trust and surrender all of myself, my efforts, and yes, even my words to Him.

As you create space for your writing and courageously take small steps forward, ushering your dreams into reality, what is God inviting you to let go of?

Pause for a few minutes and hold the question before Him.

*Papa God, Jesus, Holy Spirit,*

*What are you inviting me to let go of and leave behind?*

As you let go, there are often gifts God has waiting for us as well. For those of us who have been disappointed and wounded in the past, receiving is sometimes even harder than letting go.

Pause for a moment and ask God, *What do you have for me to receive and bring into this new season and space?*

# Dawn

## God's Gift to Writers

Joseph stood in court and interpreted with confidence because he knew that the insight He received was from God.

It was not a Joseph gift.

It was a God gift.

We can enjoy the process and do our best work when we remember from whom our gifts and writing flow. God invites us to be His vessels and become part of His creative stream. We need the divine to interpret our dreams.

It begins with us feeling safe enough to dream.

God longs to dream with us.

Will we trust Him enough to dream, and then allow Him to interpret our dreams as we step out and write in faith?

# What's Next?



I wish I could end this book with the assurance so many coaches and courses promise. Do these three things or take these five steps and you will be a best-selling author.

It's not always that simple.

Yes! We can learn from experts, take courses, strengthen our skills, experiment, stay curious, and try what experts suggest.

But there is more. God wants to use the process of writing your books to shape you and speak to you.

We want assurances that our investment of time and money will see an equal or greater return. I want this for you too.

But what if the return on writing your memoir is deeper conversations with loved ones and a stranger stumbling across your message twenty years from now in a thrift store…and it changes their life? Sometimes God calls us to work that may not seem profitable at the moment, and yet He sees the eternal impact of our writing on us, our loved ones, and the world.

Will we trust Him in the journey?

When we do, there are so many gifts from God waiting for us along the writing journey:

- our ideas
- the desire to write
- the way writing slows us down and helps us stay present
- the accomplishment of sharing our words with others
- the stillness and settledness of paying attention
- the joy of having written
- the impact of our words on immediate family and friends
- knowing we are using our gift with words
- the gratitude of holding your first book in your hands, and each one after that
- the awe of discovering that God is working through your words and stories
- selling books
- the healing that writing can bring to the writer and the readers
- unexpected gifts of insight
- a deeper connection to God when we invite Him to write with us
- and so much more!

So the question remaining is, will you write despite

    ☐ detours
    ☐ discouragement
    ☐ delays
    ☐ deterrents
    ☐ disruptions
    ☐ dark nights
    ☐ disasters?

No one else can answer this for you.

Will you choose to be an unstoppable writer?

If you said yes, take a moment to brainstorm what being an unstoppable writer means to you.

## Next Steps

Remember, all you must do is take the next step. The smaller you make your next step, the more likely you are to take it. Keep it simple.

Dream big and tackle big projects, but first break them down into small steps and mini goals.

The tallest mountains are scaled one step at a time and the same goes for making your dreams a reality. Remember, God wants to write with you!

Here is His gentle invitation to you:

Beloved,

Bring me every moment, spark,
emotion, vision, and dream.

You are mine.

I am writing your story
which began before you were born.

Your name is written
in the palm of my hand.

Remember, you were created
from the depths of me:
from my heart, my soul,
all of me.

You are my beloved,
my chosen.

Come close to me and
let's walk in the garden of your life
even if it is a desert that you have neglected.

I am with you.
I will never stop seeking you.
You and your story are MINE.

# CONCLUSION

**If this book has encouraged you, please leave a review on Amazon.** Each review increases the publicity of this book and its message. The world is in desperate need of writers, artists, and speakers dedicated to serving a higher purpose.

If you are ready to join an online writing group focused on these principles, go to:
http://www.facebook.com/groups/unstoppablewriters

If you have questions or feedback, I'd love to hear from you. Simply email welshdeanne@gmail.com.

This book is a physical reminder of God's calling and a few of the lessons He has taught me since I said "yes" to His call to write when I was twelve years old.

It has been over thirty years of wandering through various vocations since then. Each position has equipped me for the next. God has taught me to trust Him with my writing. He is my mentor and muse. I love working with writers ready to take the next step, whether it is beginning to write consistently, launching a blog, or strategically stepping up and creating a sustainable income.

You can find me at www.DeanneWelsh.com or on Facebook at
http://www.facebook.com/deannewelshwrites.

# Join Unstoppable Writers

**Are you longing to be encouraged and equipped as a writer?**

I've created a free Facebook group, **Unstoppable Writers**, where you can connect with other committed writers: http://www.facebook.com/groups/unstoppablewriters

I would love to hear from you and do my best to reply to every email: welshdeanne@gmail.com.

Take a moment to shoot me an email and tell me how your writing journey is going. If you're not feeling particularly encouraged in this season, tell me that too.

We are stronger together.

You can find me at www.DeanneWelsh.com or on Facebook and Instagram **@deannewelshwrites**

If you are longing for personalized support, I also offer spiritual direction, group coaching and one-to-one coaching for writers.

# About the Author

**Deanne Welsh** is an author, marketing strategist, and spiritual director. She is passionate about equipping writers to confidently write and share their words with the world. The author of five books, Deanne is a relentless encourager of others who loves a good laugh, pretty journals, and spending time in nature.

She has fifteen years of marketing and copywriting experience. She is a sought-after storyteller and equips her clients (writers, artists, and nonprofit ministries) to share their stories with magnetic messaging and a powerful online presence.

Her extensive experience in client relations and managing projects highlights her ability to strategically streamline processes and effectively bring out the best in others.

She is the founder and president of **Unstoppable Writers**, a writing community focused on equipping faith-focused writers to market and monetize themselves and their books. She is known for her series *Writing with God*, which examines the journey of a writer from doubt to confidence.

# APPENDIX

## Listening Prayer*

Each morning, I open my fifty-cent composition book and begin to freewrite. No editing. No judging.

Most of my entries begin with, "A new day has begun" or "Another day…"

My emotions, thoughts, experiences, and questions all find their way to the page. Whether I'm struggling to think clearly, *I feel foggy-brained and out of it today…* or baring honest confessions, *I don't know what I'm doing.*

When my mind stops scurrying, and I am done getting my thoughts onto the paper, I pause.

Taking a few deep breaths to quiet my thoughts, I whisper, *I am ready to hear from you.*

The three questions I continually return to are

- *Father God, what do you say?*
- *Jesus, what do you say?*
- *Holy Spirit, what do you say?*

*This section is an excerpt from *When God Calls a Writer* by Deanne Welsh.

I write one of these questions on the top of a new page. After asking a question, I close my eyes and wait.

As I sit in silence, I pay attention to the words, pictures, and verses that come to mind.

I write my name and then begin transcribing the pictures and words. Although I was raised in the church, I never thought God would want direct and daily communication with me. It takes courage and faith to trust that He wants such a deep and meaningful connection with me. Yet I have only to look at Jesus to see that it is true.

In the year since beginning this practice of listening prayer and restorative writing, I have been transformed.

This book is the result of listening prayer and restorative writing.

He has given me the courage to write, start online writing retreats, and serve in a deeper and more significant way than I would have chosen on my own.

He has catapulted me to connections and opportunities I previously withdrew and hid from.

He unleashed my voice when it was under an invisible weight of silence, self-hatred, and never feeling good enough.

As you write, pray, and listen, I know He will do the same for you.

Your calling and ministry will look different from mine because each person is called to a specific and unique role, but as you listen, He will guide you.

On the next page is an example of the words God placed on my heart as I paused and listened to Him.

Dearest,

You are valued. I will reveal and speak…not always before you move forward but know that even the deepest disappointment and failures you face are opportunities.

I am the most creatively saturated being. I create life from the void, something from nothing.

I speak every language and know every heart. I know the stories and experiences that will allow people to see and hear. I interpret even the wrongly worded and use even the most broken and shattered of vessels for my glory.

You can always rely on Me when I say "go" or "stop." You can trust my guidance every single time. I will make a way through the sea and calm the storm. I turn situations around in the blink of an eye.

Communication with Me is not wasted: requests, gratitude, lament…. bring them all to me. Being close to Me is the safest place to be.

Never be too busy to stop and listen to Me. This is what Martin Luther knew when he said he would spend even more time praying on his busiest days.

You can trust Me,
Jesus.

---

## Now it's your turn:

---

## Morning Pages

I stumbled across this writing practice while reading
Julia Cameron's book *The Artist's Way*. She describes
morning pages as the practice of writing three pages by
hand each morning.

The purpose is to write our stream of consciousness
and just see what flows out. It is a great tool to ground
us, cultivate self-awareness, and unleash our voice.

Writing this way, without editing, creates a space on
the page for us to express ourselves without judgment.
It can free us as writers and artists.

I've made this practice a part of my writing rhythm for
years and played with the format. For almost a year, I
used the browser app Julia created,
https://morningpages.app/. Recently I reverted to
paper and pen for a deeper body connection as I write.

Sometimes I get up early to write my morning pages
and other times I do it when I can, after hitting snooze
and dropping my son off at school. I've even written
my morning pages in the evening when my days felt
too full.

I encourage you to give it a try. This practice has been a
sacred place for me to process and where some of my
best ideas and work bubble up.

My twist on morning pages is that I begin with stream-of-consciousness writing and then I move into listening prayer. Sitting quietly, reading Scripture, and asking God to speak.

It continues to amaze me. He has so much to say to us, if only we'd stop and listen.

# Other Books by Deanne Welsh

*Writing with God* series:

BOOK 1
*When God Calls a Writer: Moving Past Insecurity to Write with Confidence*

BOOK 2 *this book
*When God Equips a Writer: Moving Past Doubt to Embrace Your Writing Destiny*

*Story by Story: The Power of a Writer*
Prompts for a 30-Day Experiment to Increase Your Impact and Improve Your Craft

*Adrift: True Stories of a Modern Mermaid*

*Living with Dragons: Break Free from the Lies Holding You Back*

Made in United States
Orlando, FL
27 December 2023

41740467R00054